Lucky Dog

Leo Butler

Published by Methuen 2004

1 3 5 7 9 10 8 6 4 2

First published in 2004 by
Methuen Publishing Limited
215 Vauxhall Bridge Road
London SW1V 1EJ

Copyright © 2004 by Leo Butler

Leo Butler has asserted his rights under the Copyright, Designs
and Patents Act, 1988, to be identified as the author of this work

Methuen Publishing Limited Reg. No. 3543167

A CIP catalogue record for this book is available from the British Library

ISBN 0 413 77466 X

Typeset by Country Setting, Kingsdown, Kent
Printed and bound in Great Britain by
Cox and Wyman Ltd, Reading, Berkshire

Caution

All rights in this play are strictly reserved.
Application for performance etc. should be made before
rehearsals begin to Michael McCoy, ICM, Oxford House,
76 Oxford Street, London W1D 1BS

No performance may be given unless a licence has been obtained.

LUCKY DOG

by **Leo Butler**

Cast in order of appearance
Eddie Webber **Alan Williams**
Sue Webber **Linda Bassett**
Brett **Liam Mills**

Director **James Macdonald**
Designer/Lighting Designer **Jean Kalman**
Sound Designer **Ian Dickinson**
Assistant Director **Maria Aberg**
Assistant Designer **Anna Calligaro**
Assistant Lighting Designer **Gavin Owen**
Casting **Lisa Makin**
Production Manager **Sue Bird**
Stage Managers **Alice Irving, Nicole Keighley,**
Stage Management Work Placement **Simon Woolley**
Costume Supervisor **Iona Kenrick**
Company Voice Work **Patsy Rodenburg**
Set built by **FIwFI**
Set Painter **Andrea Bond**
Video Imagery **Allan Parker**

The Royal Court would like to thank the following for their help with this production: Tesco UK, Waitrose.

THE COMPANY

Leo Butler (writer)

For the Royal Court: Redundant, Made of Stone.
Other theatre includes: Devotion (Theatre Centre).
Television includes: Jerusalem the Golden.
Awards include: Peggy Ramsay Foundation Award
for Individual Writing 1999, and the George Devine
Award 2001 for Redundant.
Leo is currently the Royal Court's resident drama-
tist, with the support of the Pearson Playwrights
bursary scheme.

Maria Aberg (assistant director)

As assistant director for the Royal Court: The
Sweetest Swing in Baseball, The Sugar Syndrome.
Other theatre includes: Shakespeare Love Songs
(Globe Theater, Neuss, Germany); Romeo & Juliet
(Malmo Dramatiska Teater, Sweden); Laughing Wild
(Friends of Italian Opera, Berlin); In the
Summerhouse (Intima Teatern, Malmo Sweden).
As director theatre includes: Duff Luck (Arcola); My
Best Friend (Central Station); A Handful of Dust
(Institute of Choreography & Dance, Cork); The
Maids (Judi Dench Theatre); The Lover (Mountview
Studio).
Maria is a senior script reader for the Royal Court.

Linda Bassett

For the Royal Court: Far Away, East is East
(co-production with Tamasha: Birmingham
Rep/tour/Theatre Royal, Stratford East), The
Recruiting Officer, Serious Money (Public Theater
NY), Aunt Dan and Lemon, Abel's Sister, Fen (Joint
Stock/tour/Public Theater NY).
Other theatre includes: Richard III, The Taming of
the Shrew (Globe); Five Kinds of Silence (Lyric
Hammersmith); The Dove (Croydon Warehouse);
The Triumph of Love (Almeida and tour); The
Clearing (Bush); Henry IV parts 1 & 2, The Theban
Plays, Artists and Admirers (RSC); The Awakening,
Out in the Open (Hampstead); Schism in England,
Juno and The Paycock, A Place with the Pigs (RNT);
The Seagull (Liverpool Playhouse); George Dandin,
Medea, Woyceck, Bald Prima Donna (Leicester
Haymarket/Liverpool Playhouse/Almeida); Falkland
Sound (Belgrade Coventry); The Cherry Orchard
(Leicester Haymarket); John Gabriel Borkman (ETT).
Television includes: A Village Affair, Bramwell, Loved
Up, Cold Light of Day, Frank Stubbs Promotes,
Skallagrig, A Touch of Frost, Love Hurts, A Small
Dance, Say Hello to the Real Dr Snide, The Bill,
Newshounds, Christmas, The Peter Principle, No
Bananas, Eastenders, Casualty, Kavanagh QC, Silent
Film, Far From the Madding Crowd, Spoonface
Steinberg, The Life & Crimes of William Palmer, Our
Mutual Friend, Out of Hours, The Brief.
Film includes: Waiting for the Moon, Leave to
Remain, Indian Summer, Oscar and Lucinda, East is
East, Beautiful People, The Martins, The Hours, Spivs,
Away Through the Woods, Calendar Girls.
Awards include: Best Actress Award Senana
Internacional de Cine Valladolid Espania, nominated
Best Actress London Evening Standard British Film
Awards, and nomination for Best Actress in the
BAFTA Awards 2000 (East is East).

Anna Calligaro (assistant designer)

Theatre as designer, includes: The Princess of the
Black Pavilion, Shakespeare and Me, Pyramus and
Thisbe, Blue window, Champagne and Men in
Shorts, An Enchanted April (Tristan Bates Theatre);
Voices of Morebath (NT studio); Arlecchino Sevitore
di Due Padroni (Venice); Taking Steps (Gatehouse);
The Misanthrope (JMK Competition); A Midsummer
Night's Dream (Cassiobury Junior School); One Flea
Spare (BAC).
As assistant designer, theatre includes: Come Out Eli
(Arcola, BAC); Finders Keepers (Livesey Museum);
Amadeus (Barbican).
Films includes: Krezi the Little Goat; Rabbit on the
Moon.

Ian Dickinson (sound designer)

For the Royal Court: Blest be the Tie, Ladybird,
Notes on Falling Leaves, Loyal Women, The Sugar
Syndrome, Blood, Playing the Victim, Fallout, Flesh
Wound, Hitchcock Blonde (& Lyric), Black Milk,
Crazyblackmuthafuckin'self, Caryl Churchill Shorts,
Imprint, Mother Teresa is Dead, Push Up, Workers
Writes, Fucking Games, Herons, Cutting Through
the Carnival.
Other theatre includes: Port (Royal Exchange,
Manchester); Night of the Soul (RSC Barbican); Eyes
of the Kappa (Gate); Crime and Punishment in
Dalston (Arcola Theatre); Search and Destroy (New
End, Hampstead); Phaedra, Three Sisters, The
Shaughraun, Writer's Cramp (Royal Lyceum,
Edinburgh); The Whore's Dream (RSC Fringe,
Edinburgh); As You Like It, An Experienced Woman
Gives Advice, Present Laughter, The Philadelphia
Story, Wolks World, Poor Superman, Martin
Yesterday, Fast Food, Coyote Ugly, Prizenight (Royal
Exchange, Manchester).
Ian is Head of Sound at the Royal Court.

Jean Kalman (designer and lighting designer)
For the Royal Court: Blasted.
Other theatre includes: The Cherry Orchard, The
Mahabharata, Woza Albert, The Tempest (Peter
Brook); Macbeth, King Lear, White Chameleon, A
Midsummer Night's Dream, The Powerbook (RNT);
Romeo and Juliet, Julius Caesar, Little Eyolf, Pericles
(RSC); The Beautiful Game (Really Useful Group,
West End).
Opera includes: La Clemenza Di Tito, Don Giovanni,
Fidelio, The Magic Flute (Glyndebourne); La Traviata,
The Turn of the Screw, Giulio Cesare (ROH);
Woyzeck (Opera North), Peter Grimes, Lohengrin,
Der Rosenkavalier, Mary Stuart, Semele, St John
Passion (ENO); Diary of One Who Vanished
(ENO/RNT); Pelleas et Melisande (WNO); Turandot,
La Boheme, Madame Butterfly, Il Tritico (De Vlaamse
Opera); Nabucco, Alcina, Les Contes D'Hoffmann,
The Cunning Little Vixen, Nozze Di Figaro (Paris);
Eugene Onegin (Venice, The Met); Dialogues des
Carmelites (Amsterdam, Milan, Paris, Japan); Elektra
(Salzburg, Florence); Jenufa (Salzburg); Don Giovanni,
Nozze Di Figaro, Ulisse (Aix en Provence); Tea
(Suntory Hall and De Nederlandse Opera); The
Magic Flute (Opera North); Otello (Teatro
Comunale, Florence); Salome (Opéra National
Paris); Don Giovanni (Met, New York).
Awards include: 1991 Olivier Award for Best
Lighting Designer for Richard III (RNT) and was
nominated in 1992 and 1993.

James Macdonald (director)
For the Royal Court: Blood, Blasted, 4.48 Psychosis,
Hard Fruit, Real Classy Affair, Cleansed,
Bailegangaire, Harry and Me, The Changing Room,
Simpatico, Peaches, Thyestes, The Terrible Voice of
Satan, Hammett's Apprentice, Putting Two and Two
Together.
Other theatre includes: Die Kopien (Berlin
Schaubühne); 4.48 Psychose (Vienna Burgtheater);
The Tempest, Roberto Zucco (RSC); The Triumph of
Love (Almeida); Love's Labour's Lost, Richard II
(Royal Exchange, Manchester); The Rivals
(Nottingham Playhouse); The Crackwalker (Gate);
The Seagull (Sheffield Crucible); Neon Gravy (RNT
Studio); Miss Julie (Oldham Coliseum); Juno and the
Paycock, Ice Cream & Hot Fudge, Romeo and Juliet,
Fool for Love, Savage/Love, Master Harold and the
Boys (Contact Theatre); Prem (BAC, Soho Poly).
Opera includes: Eugene Onegin, Rigoletto (WNO);
Die Zauberflöte (Garsington); Wolf Club Village;
Night Banquet (Almeida Opera); Oedipus Rex;
Survivor from Warsaw (Royal Exchange/ Hallé); Lives
of the Great Poisoners (Second Stride).
James has been an Associate Director of the Royal
Court since 1992. He is currently on a NESTA
Fellowship.

Liam Mills
Theatre includes: The Sound of Music, Scrooge, The
King and I (Tameside Hippodrome); Oliver (Oldham
Coliseum); Let the People Sing (New Mills Art
Theatre); Around the World in Song (Shaw Theatre).
Televison appearances include: GMTV, Disney Award,
Disney Channel, and various adverts.
Radio appearances include: Phil Wood's Christmas
Show, Radio Revolution.

Alan Williams
For the Royal Court: Under the Whaleback,
Terrorism, Black Milk, Crave (Paines Plough and
Bright Ltd tour), Local, Bed of Roses, Weekend After
Next (Hull Truck tour).
Other theatre includes: Casanova (tour); The Inland
Sea (Oxford Stage Company); The Sea (Chichester
Festival); The Jew of Malta (Almeida & tour); The Rib
Cage, To the Chicago Abyss (Royal Exchange,
Manchester); Kiss the Sky (Bush); Vigil (Arts Club
Theatre, Vancouver); The Darling Family (Theatre
Passe Muraille, Toronto); White Dogs of Texas
(Tarragon Theatre, Toronto & tour); The Cockroach
Trilogy (Hull Truck tour UK/US/Canada); Having a
Ball (Liverpool Playhouse); Mean Streaks (Hull Truck
tour/Bush); Small Ads (King's Head); Mary Barnes
(Birmingham Rep); Prejudice, Eejits (Liverpool
Everyman); Bridget's House (Hull Truck tour).
Television includes: Peterloo, Serious and Organised,
Paradise Heights, Wire in the Blood, Sirens, The Bill,
Peak Practice, Coronation Street, The Mayor of
Casterbridge, Love in a Cold Climate, Badger, Always
& Everyone, Touching Evil, Getting Hurt, The Scold's
Bridle, Wycliffe, Life Begins, Charles III.
Film includes: Mike Leigh Untitled 2003, The Life &
Death of Peter Sellers, Le Voyage, Cromwell &
Fairfax, Bright Young Things, Heartlands, All or
Nothing, Elephant Juice, Among Giants, The
Cockroach that Ate Cincinnati, Coleslaw,
Warehouse, The Darling Family, Daughters of the
Country.
Radio includes: Five Letters Home to Elizabeth,
Hard Time.

THE ENGLISH STAGE COMPANY AT THE ROYAL COURT

The English Stage Company at the Royal Court opened in 1956 as a subsidised theatre producing new British plays, international plays and some classical revivals.

The first artistic director George Devine aimed to create a writers' theatre, 'a place where the dramatist is acknowledged as the fundamental creative force in the theatre and where the play is more important than the actors, the director, the designer'. The urgent need was to find a contemporary style in which the play, the acting, direction and design are all combined. He believed that 'the battle will be a long one to continue to create the right conditions for writers to work in'.

Devine aimed to discover 'hard-hitting, uncompromising writers whose plays are stimulating, provocative and exciting'. The Royal Court production of John Osborne's Look Back in Anger in May 1956 is now seen as the decisive starting point of modern British drama and the policy created a new generation of British playwrights. The first wave included John Osborne, Arnold Wesker, John Arden, Ann Jellicoe, N F Simpson and Edward Bond. Early seasons included new international plays by Bertolt Brecht, Eugène Ionesco, Samuel Beckett, Jean-Paul Sartre and Marguerite Duras.

The theatre started with the 400-seat proscenium arch Theatre Downstairs, and in 1969 opened a second theatre, the 60-seat studio Theatre Upstairs. Some productions transfer to the West End, such as Terry Johnson's Hitchcock Blonde, Caryl Churchill's Far Away, Conor McPherson's The Weir, Kevin Elyot's Mouth to Mouth and My Night With Reg. The Royal Court also co-produces plays which have transferred to the West End or toured internationally, such as Sebastian Barry's The Steward of Christendom and Mark Ravenhill's Shopping and Fucking (with Out of Joint), Martin McDonagh's The Beauty Queen Of Leenane (with Druid Theatre Company), Ayub Khan Din's East is East (with Tamasha Theatre Company, and now a feature film).

Since 1994 the Royal Court's artistic policy has again been vigorously directed to finding and producing a new generation of playwrights. The writers include Joe Penhall, Rebecca Prichard, Michael Wynne, Nick Grosso, Judy Upton, Meredith Oakes, Sarah Kane, Anthony Neilson, Judith Johnson, James Stock, Jez Butterworth, Marina Carr, Phyllis Nagy, Simon Block, Martin McDonagh, Mark Ravenhill, Ayub Khan Din, Tamantha Hammerschlag, Jess Walters, Ché Walker, Conor McPherson,

photo: Andy Chopping

Simon Stephens, Richard Bean, Roy Williams, Gary Mitchell, Mick Mahoney, Rebecca Gilman, Christopher Shinn, Kia Corthron, David Gieselmann, Marius von Mayenburg, David Eldridge, Leo Butler, Zinnie Harris, Grae Cleugh, Roland Schimmelpfennig, DeObia Oparei, Vassily Sigarev, the Presnyakov Brothers and Lucy Prebble. This expanded programme of new plays has been made possible through the support of A.SK Theater Projects and the Skirball Foundation, the Jerwood Charitable Foundation, the American Friends of the Royal Court Theatre and many in association with the Royal National Theatre Studio.

In recent years there have been record-breaking productions at the box office, with capacity houses for Roy Williams' Fallout, Terry Johnson's Hitchcock Blonde, Caryl Churchill's A Number, Jez Butterworth's The Night Heron, Rebecca Gilman's Boy Gets Girl, Kevin Elyot's Mouth to Mouth, David Hare's My Zinc Bed and Conor McPherson's The Weir, which transferred to the West End in October 1998 and ran for nearly two years at the Duke of York's Theatre.

The newly refurbished theatre in Sloane Square opened in February 2000, with a policy still inspired by the first artistic director George Devine. The Royal Court is an international theatre for new plays and new playwrights, and the work shapes contemporary drama in Britain and overseas.

AWARDS FOR ROYAL COURT

Jez Butterworth won the 1995 George Devine Award, the Writers' Guild New Writer of the Year Award, the Evening Standard Award for Most Promising Playwright and the Olivier Award for Best Comedy for Mojo.

The Royal Court was the overall winner of the 1995 Prudential Award for the Arts for creativity, excellence, innovation and accessibility. The Royal Court Theatre Upstairs won the 1995 Peter Brook Empty Space Award for innovation and excellence in theatre.

Michael Wynne won the 1996 Meyer-Whitworth Award for The Knocky. Martin McDonagh won the 1996 George Devine Award, the 1996 Writers' Guild Best Fringe Play Award, the 1996 Critics' Circle Award and the 1996 Evening Standard Award for Most Promising Playwright for The Beauty Queen of Leenane. Marina Carr won the 19th Susan Smith Blackburn Prize (1996/7) for Portia Coughlan. Conor McPherson won the 1997 George Devine Award, the 1997 Critics' Circle Award and the 1997 Evening Standard Award for Most Promising Playwright for The Weir. Ayub Khan Din won the 1997 Writers' Guild Awards for Best West End Play and Writers' Guild New Writer of the Year and the 1996 John Whiting Award for East is East (co-production with Tamasha).

At the 1998 Tony Awards, Martin McDonagh's The Beauty Queen of Leenane (co-production with Druid Theatre Company) won four awards including Garry Hynes for Best Director and was nominated for a further two. Eugene Ionesco's The Chairs (co-production with Theatre de Complicite) was nominated for six Tony awards. David Hare won the 1998 Time Out Live Award for Outstanding Achievement and six awards in New York including the Drama League, Drama Desk and New York Critics Circle Award for Via Dolorosa. Sarah Kane won the 1998 Arts Foundation Fellowship in Playwriting. Rebecca Prichard won the 1998 Critics' Circle Award for Most Promising Playwright for Yard Gal (co-production with Clean Break).

Conor McPherson won the 1999 Olivier Award for Best New Play for The Weir. The Royal Court won the 1999 ITI Award for Excellence in International Theatre. Sarah Kane's Cleansed was judged Best Foreign Language Play in 1999 by Theater Heute in Germany. Gary Mitchell won the 1999 Pearson Best Play Award for Trust. Rebecca Gilman was joint winner of the 1999 George Devine Award and won the 1999 Evening Standard Award for Most Promising Playwright for The Glory of Living.

In 1999, the Royal Court won the European theatre prize New Theatrical Realities, presented at Taormina Arte in Sicily, for its efforts in recent years in discovering and producing the work of young British dramatists.

Roy Williams and Gary Mitchell were joint winners of the George Devine Award 2000 for Most Promising Playwright for Lift Off and The Force of Change respectively. At the Barclays Theatre Awards 2000 presented by the TMA, Richard Wilson won the Best Director Award for David Gieselmann's Mr Kolpert and Jeremy Herbert won the Best Designer Award for Sarah Kane's 4.48 Psychosis. Gary Mitchell won the Evening Standard's Charles Wintour Award 2000 for Most Promising Playwright for The Force of Change. Stephen Jeffreys' I Just Stopped by to See the Man won an AT&T: On Stage Award 2000.

David Eldridge's Under the Blue Sky won the Time Out Live Award 2001 for Best New Play in the West End. Leo Butler won the George Devine Award 2001 for Most Promising Playwright for Redundant. Roy Williams won the Evening Standard's Charles Wintour Award 2001 for Most Promising Playwright for Clubland. Grae Cleugh won the 2001 Olivier Award for Most Promising Playwright for Fucking Games. Richard Bean was joint winner of the George Devine Award 2002 for Most Promising Playwright for Under the Whaleback. Caryl Churchill won the 2002 Evening Standard Award for Best New Play for A Number. Vassily Sigarev won the 2002 Evening Standard Charles Wintour Award for Most Promising Playwright for Plasticine. Ian MacNeil won the 2002 Evening Standard Award for Best Design for A Number and Plasticine. Peter Gill won the 2002 Critics' Circle Award for Best New Play for The York Realist (English Touring Theatre). Ché Walker won the 2003 George Devine Award for Most Promising Playwright for Flesh Wound. Lucy Prebble won the 2003 Critics' Circle Award for Most Promising Playwright for The Sugar Syndrome.

ROYAL COURT BOOKSHOP

The Royal Court bookshop offers a diverse selection of contemporary plays and publications on the theory and practice of modern drama. The staff specialise in assisting with the selection of audition monologues and scenes.
Royal Court playtexts from past and present productions cost £2.
The Bookshop is situated in the downstairs ROYAL COURT BAR AND FOOD.
Monday–Friday 3–10pm, Saturday 2–10pm
For information tel: 020 7565 5024
or email: bookshop@royalcourttheatre.com

PROGRAMME SUPPORTERS

The Royal Court (English Stage Company Ltd) receives its principal funding from Arts Council England, London. It is also supported financially by a wide range of private companies and public bodies and earns the remainder of its income from the box office and its own trading activities. The Royal Borough of Kensington & Chelsea gives an annual grant to the Royal Court Young Writers Programme.

The Genesis Foundation supports the International Season and Young Writers Festival.

The Jerwood Charity supports new plays by new playwrights through the Jerwood New Playwrights series. The Skirball Foundation funds a Playwrights' Programme at the theatre. The Artistic Director's Chair is supported by a lead grant from The Peter Jay Sharp Foundation, contributing to the activities of the Artistic Director's office. Bloomberg Mondays, the Royal Court's reduced price ticket scheme, is supported by Bloomberg. Over the past eight years the BBC has supported the Gerald Chapman Fund for directors.

Association of
London Government

JERWOOD
NEW PLAYWRIGHTS

Since 1993 Jerwood New Playwrights have contributed to some of the Royal Court's most successful productions, including SHOPPING AND FUCKING by Mark Ravenhill (co-production with Out of Joint), EAST IS EAST by Ayub Khan Din (co-production with Tamasha), THE BEAUTY QUEEN OF LEENANE by Martin McDonagh (co-production with Druid Theatre Company), THE WEIR by Conor McPherson, REAL CLASSY AFFAIR by Nick Grosso, THE FORCE OF CHANGE by Gary Mitchell, ON RAFTERY'S HILL by Marina Carr (co-production with Druid Theatre Company), 4.48 PSYCHOSIS by Sarah Kane, UNDER THE BLUE SKY by David Eldridge, PRESENCE by David Harrower, HERONS by Simon Stephens, CLUBLAND by Roy Williams, REDUNDANT by Leo Butler, NIGHTINGALE AND CHASE by Zinnie Harris, FUCKING GAMES by Grae Cleugh, BEDBOUND by Enda Walsh, THE PEOPLE ARE FRIENDLY by Michael Wynne, OUTLYING ISLANDS by David Greig and IRON by Rona Munro, UNDER THE WHALEBACK by Richard Bean, FLESH WOUND by Ché Walker, FALL-OUT by Roy Williams, FOOD CHAIN by Mick Mahoney and NOTES ON FALLING LEAVES by Ayub Khan Din. This season Jerwood New Playwrights are supporting LUCKY DOG by Leo Butler and COUNTRY MUSIC by Simon Stephens.

The Jerwood Charity is a registered charity dedicated to imaginative and responsible funding and sponsorship of the arts, education, design and other areas of human endeavour and excellence.

HERONS by Simon Stephens
(photo: Pete Jones)

EAST IS EAST by Ayub Khan Din
(photo: Robert Day)

Lucky Dog

For Nazzi

Characters

Eddie Webber, fifty-seven years old
Sue Webber, fifty-eight years old
Brett, ten years old

Settings

Scenes One to Three: Eddie and Sue's house in Sheffield. Christmas night.

Scenes Four to Ten: a beach in Fuerteventura, the Canary Islands. One year later, day.

Acknowledgements

I'd like to thank Graham Whybrow, Ian Rickson and James Macdonald, without whom I could not have completed this play.

Thanks also to Ola and the team at the YWP for letting me use the writers' room, for their enthusiasm, and for generously putting up with the cigarette smoke.

LB, April 2004

One

Christmas Day. 5.00 p.m.

Eddie *and* **Sue** *sitting at the table eating Christmas dinner.*

Silence.

Sue   Where'd yer take 'er?

Eddie   Nowhere. Around. Up woods n' back.

Sue   Won't eat 'er giblets.

Eddie   She will.

Sue   Can hardly stand, poor thing.

Silence.

Didn't hear yer leave. Were up n' about by eight. Must've left very early.

Eddie   Not really.

Sue   Had me worried, not a word all day. Thought yer might be in some bother.

Eddie   No.

Sue   Thought yer might be gone for good.

Silence.

Eddie   Took 'er round park.

Sue   Oh.

Eddie   Round park f' ten minutes.

Sue   Guessed as much.

Eddie   Down Crabtree Pond. Up through woods. Over heliport n' back

Sue   You work that dog too hard.

Eddie   She's alright.

Sue   Paw marks all over the carpet.

Eddie   She's not bothered.

Sue   Only bathed 'er Sunday, state of 'er already.

Silence.

Save me some o' them parsnips, won't yer?

Silence.

Many up there?

Eddie   Few.

Sue   That's nice.

Eddie   Couple o' terriers.

Sue   Oh.

Eddie   Staff.

Sue   Not many then.

Eddie   Not many. No.

Silence.

Retriever.

Sue   What?

Eddie   Golden retriever. Cone round its neck. Stop it scratchin'.

Sue   Oh dear.

Eddie   Skin infection.

Sue   Oh dear.

Silence.

Hope yer washed yer hands.

Eddie   Saw a robin.

Sue   What?

Eddie   Robin redbreast. Perched on bench by playground. Had to put 'er on lead, stop 'er chasin' it away. Tiny little thing.

Sue   Thought yer might've popped round Pam's.

Eddie   Ay.

Sue   Lovely fit.

Silence.

Does wonders f' yer waistline.

Eddie   Does it?

Sue   Seen it meself, in the window. TK Max. One o' the bargains.

Eddie   Oh.

Sue   In the bargain bin. Didn't think it were quite you. Didn't think it were quite your style.

Eddie   Didn't know I 'ad a style.

Sue   Not of yer own choosin', no.

Silence.

Very thoughtful of 'er.

Eddie   Ay.

Sue   Wunt want t' catch a chill.

Eddie   I won't.

Sue   How's she copin'?

Eddie   Oh. Yer know. Copin'.

Sue   You t' keep 'er company.

Silence.

Must be 'ard. This time o' year. All on 'er own.

Eddie   Dint mention it.

Sue   At her age.

Silence.

Eddie *pulls a Christmas card out of his back-pocket. He takes it out of its envelope and places it in the middle of the table.*

Eddie *eats.*

Silence.

Sue *takes the Chrsitmas card and examines it.*

Silence.

Good of her.

Eddie   Passed on yer regards.

Sue *places the Christmas card back on the table.*

Silence.

Sue   Hang it wi' the others can't we? Plenty o' room on the line.

Eddie   That's what it's there for.

Sue   That's what I thought.

Eddie   That's what it's there for.

Silence.

Sue   Had to put the caulies in wi' the sprouts. Used up every dish in the house.

Eddie   Oh.

Sue   Left it any longer they'd've turned t' bloody mush. 'Ad this thing on fifty degrees since three. Worried it might be too crisp.

Eddie   Nice n' tender.

Sue   D'yer want my skin?

Eddie   Ay.

Sue   Pass us yer plate.

Silence.

More gravy in the boat if yer want it.

Silence.

Yer missed the Queen's speech.

Eddie Oh.

Sue Yer didn't miss much. Yer know what she's like.

Silence.

Shed a few pounds since the op.

Eddie Be dead come summer.

Sue Expect she's got 'er hands full today. William n' Harry, bless. Squabbles round the table.

Eddie Ay.

Sue All the same at that age aren't they? Who gets to wear Granny's crown. Disappearing to their rooms every five minutes. The noise.

Silence.

Footsteps on the landin'.

Silence.

Surprised she's got the time f' the BBC.

Eddie It's 'im.

Sue What?

Eddie Blair.

Sue What about 'im?

Eddie Do owt 'e bloody well says, she will.

Sue Won't 'ear a word said against that man.

Eddie . . .

Sue Not today.

Eddie (*mumbles*) Bloody poodle.

Sue What?

Silence.

Mumble.

Silence.

Weather says it's goin' t' snow tomorrow. If the weather's good.

Silence.

Thought we might drive over Chatsworth. Stop by that pub does the Ploughman's.

Silence.

Sue   She'd like that.

Eddie   She would.

Sue   Put me wellies on, could walk 'er down the caves. Ladybower. Do us good, a change of scenery.

Silence.

Wear yer new whatsit.

Eddie   What?

Sue   What-yer-call-it.

Eddie   Fleece.

Sue   Wear it in.

Eddie   Ay.

Sue   Nothin' planned?

Silence.

I said yer've nothin' planned.

Eddie   No.

Sue   Well. That's settled then.

Silence.

Sue   Sure yer not too hot in that thing?

Silence.

Oh . . . Almost forgot.

Sue *offers* **Eddie** *her Christmas cracker.*

Sue M an' S. They're ever so posh. Marks an' Sparks, look, come on.

Eddie *pulls* **Sue***'s cracker.*

Sue Leave it t' you we'd be recylin' last year's.

Sue *puts on her Christmas hat.*

Sue Well? What d'yer think?

Silence.

'Ere.

Sue *takes* **Eddie***'s cracker.*

Sue 'Ant paid nine ninety-nine f' you t' just sit there, come on. Come on, Ted.

Eddie *takes his cracker,* **Sue** *takes the other end.*

They pull – it pops.

Eddie *puts his hat on.*

Silence.

Sue Still another ten in box.

Silence.

Yer don't have to wear that one.

Eddie I want to wear this one.

Sue I'm just sayin' . . .

Eddie What?

Sue Yer don't have to wear that one.

Eddie It's fine.

Sue Sat there, pullin' faces . . .

Eddie I said it's fine.

Silence.

Sue *takes her joke.*

Sue   What did the envelope say to the stamp?

Silence.

Stick with me n' we'll go places.

Silence.

Sue *takes the joke from* **Eddie***'s cracker.*

Sue   How do snails keep their shells shiny?

Silence.

Snail polish.

Silence.

Sue *looks through the contents of her cracker.*

Sue   Oh. It's a puzzle, look.

Sue *opens the small plastic puzzle, unrolls the instructions.*

Sue *examines the instructions.*

Sue   Think yer meant to piece it together.

Sue *tries sticking the pieces together.*

Sue   Can't be right. I think this bit sticks to this bit . . .

Sue *continues.*

Sue   No. No, I don't think . . .

Sue *continues.*

Sue   Ah. That's it. There, look – it's a . . .

The toy falls apart.

It's supposed to spin. It's a spinny thing.

Eddie *takes the toy and fixes it.*

He passes it back to **Sue***.*

Spin it.

Sue   What?

Eddie   Spin it.

Sue   No need t' shout.

Eddie   . . .

Sue   I know what I'm doin'.

Sue *spins the toy.*

It spins off the table.

Silence.

Sue   Bit o' fun.

Silence.

What did you get?

Sue *takes* **Eddie***'s cracker, empties it out.*

She pulls out a plastic bracelet.

Sue   Oh now.

Sue *takes the plastic bracelet out of it's wrapper.*

Sue   Now that's more like it.

Sue *puts the bracelet on.*

Sue   Look.

Silence.

They eat.

Silence.

He called.

Eddie   What?

Sue   He called.

Silence.

Nice to 'ear a friendly voice. Said there's still time if yer want to change yer mind. Still a few hours before bedtime.

Silence.

Don't worry about yer father n' me I said. Quite happy t'
keep ourselves occupied for one year. Up to me eyes wi'the
bloody turkey as it is. One year won't hurt.

Eddie   No.

Sue   Do as yer please, I said. Long as you're happy.

Silence.

Said yer'd give 'im a ring later. Once we're settled.

Silence.

Sue   Special on tonight.

Eddie   What?

Sue   *Only Fools n' Horses.* It's a Christmas special. Del-Boy
comes up with a plan to make some money. He doesn't
want anythin' to do with it, Rodney I mean. He knows it'll
only spell trouble. Course 'e's right. It all goes wrong in the
end.

Silence.

Looks hysterical on the advert.

Silence.

Yer will call 'im, won't yer, Ted? He'll be ever so sad if yer
don't. Yer will though, won't yer?

Eddie   Yes.

Silence.

Sue   Well. He had his dinner at two and . . .

Sue *checks her watch.*

Sue   Oh. Should be there be now. Off to 'er uncle's. Her
great uncle. On 'er daddy's side. In his nineties, bless. Lives
way across the other side of the city 'e said. Been there since
the fifties. Bit of a convoy. All the grandkids, the whole
family – must be what? Twenty, twenty-five of 'em all in all.

All in their cars, over the River Thames n' back. Every year apparently. Somethin' of a tradition. Sounded very busy over the phone – Well, yer'll hear. Hardly get a word o' sense out of 'im. Says they've taken to 'im though. Even with the noise, 'e says they're all very kind.

Silence.

They've offered t' pay f' the weddng.

Eddie   What?

Sue   'Er father. He's written them a cheque.

Eddie   'Ow much?

Sue   Sounds quite the character. Just cracked open the bubbly when he called. Ten o'clock in the mornin'.

Eddie   'Ow much?

Sue   Hardly settin' an example are they?

Silence.

He didn't say.

Silence.

They've got a piano.

Eddie   Good.

Sue   Said he has to have a singalong later. Yer know what he's like. Him. Givin' it 'Jingle Bells'. Haven't heard a note out of 'im since 'e were three year old. Said yer'd better start practisin', love. Said yer'd better make the most o' that champagne while there's time. Have a brandy or two, God 'elp us.

Eddie   He'll be fine.

Sue   Course he's bound to have a few.

Eddie   Ay.

Sue   No stoppin' 'im usually.

Silence.

Under the table last year.

Eddie *chuckles.*

Sue   With his hat on.

Eddie *and* **Sue** *both chuckle.*

Sue (*chuckling*)   The bloody . . . The whatsit . . . The . . .

Eddie *laughs.*

Sue   Round his ankles . . .

Sue *laughs,* **Eddie** *laughs.*

Sue   Still got the picture.

Silence.

Eddie *and* **Sue** *eat.*

Silence.

Sue   Give what yer can though, don't yer?

Eddie   Ay.

Sue   Every little helps.

Silence.

Over the moon with his Diskman.

Eddie   What?

Sue   We sent 'im a Diskman.

Eddie   Oh.

Sue   He told me t' tell yer. Over the moon.

Eddie   Right.

Sue   Take it with 'im on the tube train. Keep 'im on 'is toes. Not just compact disks neither. Tune into Radio Four if 'e wants. Five Live f' the sport. Thinkin' o' gettin' one meself.

Eddie   Make a start.

Sue   What?

Eddie   Tomorrow. Get that gate fixed up out back.

Sue   Been sayin' that f' weeks.

Eddie   Pick up some hinges.

Sue   Shops aren't open till Friday.

Eddie   Done be lunchtime.

Sue   Weather says it's goin' t' snow.

Eddie   Stop 'er gettin' ideas. Stop 'er runnin' off.

Sue   Be good t' get out the 'ouse, Ted.

Silence.

Didn't know yer liked Neil Young.

Eddie   What?

Sue   The album they bought yer.

Eddie   Yes I do.

Sue   Well, I didn't know. Yer've never mentioned it to me. Yer've never expressed an opinion.

Silence.

Then yer wouldn't, would yer?

Eddie   No.

Sue   Not to me anyway.

Silence.

What?

Eddie   Somethin' I 'eard.

Sue   Somethin' you heard.

Eddie   Somethin' someone told me.

Sue   I see.

Silence.

Wear it on the day, can't I?

Eddie   What?

Sue   Go well with me frock, won't it?

Eddie   Right.

Sue   Go well with me frock.

Silence.

Sue *removes the bracelet from her wrist.*

Sue *puts the bracelet back in its plastic wrapper.*

Silence.

Sue   Wouldn't want to upstage the bride though, would I?

Silence.

Sue *pours wine and drinks.*

Silence.

Sue   She's very good for 'im, though.

Eddie   Ay.

Sue   She's a very good influence, I mean. Pair of 'em together, they'll rule the bloody world time they're forty.

Eddie   If yer say so.

Sue   Quite a looker.

Eddie   What?

Sue   Said so yerself. The quiet type. Hardly get a word out of 'er on the phone. She's quite a looker, yer said.

Eddie   Did I?

Sue   Told me she looked like Catherine Zeta Jones.

Eddie   When?

Sue   Barely took yer eyes off the poor girl. Small wonder she's so shy, you gawpin'.

Silence.

Thought they might've driven up.

Eddie   Ay.

Sue   Driven up f' Boxin' Day at least.

Silence.

Scared 'er off.

Eddie   What?

Sue   I said yer must've scared 'er away.

Silence.

Sat there like Stone'enge.

Silence.

Funny.

Eddie   What is?

Sue   Hard to imagine he'd ever settle down. Take after yer father, I said to 'im. 'E were just the same when we first met. All that ambition. All that hair.

Silence.

Always thought yer'd end up shacked up in some commune, savin' the bloody . . .

Eddie *grabs the carving knife.*

Sue   What?

Eddie *carves off a turkey leg.*

Sue   Eddie . . .

Pause.

Eddie, don't.

Eddie *takes the turkey leg and puts it in the dish with the roast potatoes.*

Sue   Use the roll. The kitchen roll . . .

Eddie *removes the left-over roast potatoes and puts them on his plate.*

Sue   Grease all over the tablecloth, be careful.

Eddie *exits with the dish.*

Sue   Spoil that dog!

Silence.

Sue *fills up her glass of white wine.*

Sue *sips.*

Silence.

Sue *drinks half the glass of white wine.*

Sue *fills up her glass again.*

Sue *sips.*

Silence.

Sue *unbuttons her top.*

Sue *checks her left breast for lumps.*

Silence.

Sue *buttons up her top.*

Silence.

Sue *swallows the wine down in one.*

Silence.

Sue *gets up out of her chair.*

Sue *serves the vegetables and the turkey carcass onto* **Eddie**'s *plate.*

Sue *sits.*

Silence.

Eddie *re-enters from the kitchen.*

Eddie *sits.*

Eddie *eats.*

Silence.

Sue   D'yer have to?

Silence.

Eddie *eats.*

Silence.

Sue   Don't do that, Eddie. Right in me 'ear.

Silence.

Eddie *finishes eating, lays his cutlery on the plate.*

Silence.

Sue   Still some left.

Eddie   Stuffed.

Sue   Not like you. Get it eaten.

Silence.

Get it eaten, I said.

Silence.

Eddie *sparks a cigarette.*

Silence.

Sue   Mind yer don't get ash all over that.

Eddie   What?

Sue   Wunt want t' ruin it. All the trouble she's gone to.

Silence.

Should call 'im.

Silence.

Don't want t' leave it too late.

Eddie   In a minute.

Silence.

Sue   I went out.

Silence.

I went out.

Eddie   Did yer?

Sue   Next door. Poked me 'ead round the door this mornin'. Dropped off their card.

Silence.

Told 'im we'd have Brett for an hour.

Eddie   What?

Sue   He's not all bad.

Eddie   He's a little bastard.

Sue   Thought we'd be doin' 'em a favour, bit o' peace. Liven this place up for a start.

Silence.

Just for an hour.

Eddie   Fine.

Sue   They've got enough t' think about with the new baby. She's only just out the hospital, f' Chrissakes.

Silence.

Said he could play with Lucky.

Eddie   You . . .?

Sue   Think she's had enough exercise for one day already.

Eddie   What time?

Sue   He's comin'.

Silence.

Might not come at all. Might be fast asleep by now, yer know what they're like at that age. Day's over by six.

Silence.

Help me put the dishes away.

Silence.

Have it done in no time, the two of us.

Eddie   Ay.

Sue   She's not expectin' yer.

Eddie   What?

Sue   Pamela. She's not . . .

Eddie   No.

Sue   Give me a hand then.

Eddie   I will.

Silence.

Sue   Nobody's forcin' yer, Ted.

Silence.

Come n' go as yer please.

Silence.

Sue *pours wine and drinks.*

Silence.

Sue   Play a game later.

Silence.

Trivial Pursuits. That's a good game. You're good at general knowledge. You are. Yer better than me, I'm hopeless.

Silence.

Bit o' fun.

Silence.

Well. Think it's almost time for . . .

The phone rings.

That'll be 'im now.

Long pause.

Well, go on.

Eddie *stubs out his cigarette.*

Eddie *gets up out of his chair.*

The phone stops ringing.

Eddie *sits back down.*

Silence.

Expect 'e'll call back later.

Sue   Expect 'e will.

Silence.

Expect 'e'll leave a message if yer give it a few . . .

Eddie   I don't love you.

Silence.

Sue   Yer entitled to yer opinion.

Silence.

Eddie   I'll do it.

Blackout.

Two

Same day. 8.00 p.m.

Brett *and* **Sue** *sitting at the table.*

Brett *reluctantly eats a dish of Christmas pudding.*

Sue *sips her wine.*

They both wear Christmas-cracker hats.

Sue   How is it?

Silence.

I made it special. Yer mummy says it's yer favourite, she told me. She talks about you a lot.

Silence.

Squirty cream.

Silence.

Make yer big n' strong. Make yer burst like a balloon.

Silence.

Just a little bit then, eh?

Sue *squirts cream onto* **Brett***'s pudding.*

Sue   It is Christmas after all.

Silence.

Oh.

Sue *pulls a dog hair out of the cream.*

Sue   One of Lucky's by the look of it.

Sue *wipes the dog hair onto a napkin, then licks her fingers clean.*

Sue   Ooh. Yummy.

Silence.

Must be very exciting. Santa bring yer lots of presents. I bet 'e did. Someone's been a good boy this year. Someone's been very lucky. Little sister t' share yer stockin' with.

Brett   S'pose.

Sue   Someone to play with.

Brett *shrugs.*

Sue   Size of yer hand, int she?

Brett   Yeah.

Sue   I've seen 'er.

Silence.

Remember when you were that age. Had to look after yer
one night. Yer don't remember, do yer? Still in nappies back
then, practically screamed the house down. Tried puttin' you
in the bath, keep yer quiet. Yer wouldn't have it. Could hear
yer half way down the street.

Silence.

Bet yer've got a fair few admirers at school now, eh?
Handsome lad like you.

Brett   No.

Sue   Seen yer out the back with yer football. Proper little
David Beckham. Must be havin' to fight 'em off. I bet you
are. I bet they're hangin' off your shorts.

Silence.

Take after yer father.

Brett   Wanna go 'ome.

Sue   Oh now . . .

Brett   Wanna go 'ome.

Sue   Yer've only just got 'ere.

Brett   Shuddup.

Sue   What did you promise?

Brett *shrugs.*

Sue   Promised t' be good.

Silence.

Promised yer mum I'd take care of yer. She's only next
door, cheer up.

Brett   Can I 'ave some Coke?

Sue   Haven't finished yer squash yet.

Brett   Mum said I could 'ave some Coke.

Sue   Everyone likes lemon squash. It's good f' yer, come on.

Brett (*mumbles*)   Tastes like pee.

Sue   What?

Brett   Nothin'.

Sue   Tastes like what?

Sue *sips the drink.*

Sue   Funny tastin' pee.

Silence.

Brett   Our tree's massive.

Sue   It is.

Brett   Yer can see ours from the park. Yours is titchy compared.

Silence.

Sue   Lovely sweater. My Danny's one just like it. When he was small like you. Stripes. He had a motorbike one year. A toy one, that is. Barry Sheen on top. Bet yer'd like one o' them. That or a racin' car.

Brett *shrugs.*

Sue   Lucky if I got an orange when I was your age. Didn't even have decorations in my house. Not with my dad. Couldn't tell if it were Christmas or Easter. Couldn't tell the difference. No one t' play with. Wouldn't like that now, would yer?

Brett   No.

Sue   Wouldn't like that at all.

Brett   Got a Gandalf.

Sue   Have yer now?

Brett   And a Gollum. They're in me drawer. They talk to each other.

Sue   Do they?

Brett *shrugs.*

Sue   Are you the Lord of the Rings?

Brett   No.

Sue   I think you are.

Brett   I'm Frodo Baggins.

Sue   What am I, then?

Brett   Nowt.

Silence.

Be a cavetroll if yer want.

Sue   Oh.

Brett   That's all that's left.

Sue   What does a cavetroll do?

Brett   Kill it.

Sue   What?.

Brett   Kill yer.

Sue   Oh.

Brett   Shoot an arrow in yer face.

Sue   Long as it's just for fun.

Brett   No.

Silence.

Sue   Sing me a carol.

Silence.

Must know a carol or two, surely. Don't they teach yer them at school? I used t' be in the choir at my school.

Silence.

Sue *sings.*

> Away in a manger,
> No crib for a bed,
> The little lord Jesus
> Laid down his sweet head.
>
> The stars in the bright sky
> Looked down where he lay,
> The little lord Jesus
> Asleep in the hay.

Brett *finishes his pudding, lays his spoon down.*

Brett   Finished now.

Sue   What d'yer say?

Brett   Thank you.

Sue   Thank you what?

Brett   Mrs Webber . . .

Sue   That's right . . .

Brett   Mrs Webber.

Sue   Good.

Brett   Mrs Webber, Mrs Webber, Mrs Webber!

Silence.

Sue   Well. Yer've done very well.

Brett   Can I play with your dog?

Sue   Oh . . .

Brett   Mum said I could play with your dog.

Sue   Afraid yer've just missed 'er, duck.

Brett   No I 'ant.

Sue   They're only round the park. Should be back in a few minutes.

Brett   But . . .

Sue   Doubt she'll be up to much playin' anyway. She's very old. Barely lift 'er out the basket once my Ted's 'ad 'is way. Be fifteen come May. That's over a hundred in dog years.

Brett   I know.

Sue   Well then.

Silence.

Play with me in the meantime, can't yer?

Silence.

So.

Silence.

How is everything? At home, I mean.

Silence.

Look under the tree, yer might find somethin' special.

Silence.

Oh.

Sue *finds a photo album on the table.*

Sue   Look what I found.

Brett   Shuddup.

Sue   Might find Lucky if we're lucky, come on.

Sue *takes the photo album and sits by* **Brett**.

She opens the album, showing **Brett** *the photographs.*

Silence.

Sue This was her when she was just a puppy. Goin' back years. 1988. See my ankle in the shot, look.

Brett *shrugs.*

Sue This one's even earlier. Alton Towers. That's my Danny in the queue for the corkscrew. Can't've been much older than you are now.

Silence.

That's the three of us on the log flume. Look at 'is little face, look.

Silence.

Lucky again. In the Lake District one summer.

Silence.

Danny at his sports day. He came third in the egg n' spoon.

Silence.

That's him in his Boy George phase. Pullin' one of 'is faces. Think he'd just had his TB jab.

Silence.

Lucky.

Silence.

Oh. Oh now. That's Danny in the school play. *Bugsy Malone.* You wouldn't recognise 'im would yer? At the back there – Can you see him?

Silence.

Him with one of his girlfriends. Don't know what ever happened to her.

Silence.

That's him on the mornin' of his GCSE results.

Silence.

That's him on the evenin' of his GCSE results.

Silence.

Looks like Neil from *The Young Ones* here. Eyes the size of saucers.

Silence.

That's him at the interchange in town. On his way down to London. On his way to university. Big strong man there i'nt 'e?

Brett *shrugs.*

Sue   You'll be as tall as that one day.

Silence.

Lucky.

Silence.

Lucky in the bath.

Silence.

Don't know what this one's meant t' be.

Silence.

Lucky again. Lickin' the lens. Big fat nose, what d'yer call it?

Brett *shrugs.*

Sue   Call it 'er snout.

Silence.

Lucky with 'er dad last year. In the park.

Silence.

Lucky with an apple on 'er head. One o' my Ted's tricks, I think.

Silence.

In 'er basket, look.

Silence.

Lucky.

Silence.

Lucky again.

Silence.

Sue *flicks through the photo album.*

Silence.

Sue *puts the photo album away.*

Silence.

Sue *pours herself a glass of wine and drinks.*

Silence.

'Ave a glass of brandy if yer'd rather.

Silence.

Christmas wunt be Christmas without a drop of brandy
or . . .

Brett   Gonna send me 'ome now?

Sue   Oh . . .

Brett   I'm bored.

Sue   Well, I don't think . . .

Brett   Yer borin'.

Sue   Think yer'd better keep them thoughts to yerself,
don't you?

Brett   Piss off.

Silence.

Sue   Know what we do with words like that?

Brett   No.

Sue   Flush 'em down the toilet f' the rats to 'ave their way.

Silence.

Wunt want to go down with 'em.

Brett   Yeah.

Sue   Down the toilet.

Brett   Better than 'ere.

Silence.

Sue   Don't yer want t' know what Santa's got yer?

Brett   I am Santa.

Sue   Well . . .

Brett   I am.

Silence.

Sue   Yer name's on it.

Silence.

Brett *climbs out of his chair and moves to the Christmas tree.*

Brett *investigates the tree.*

Sue   Good boy.

Brett *grabs the angel off the top of the tree.*

Sue   Brett!

Brett   Where's 'er eyes gone?

Sue   Yer'll break it!

Brett   She 'ant got no eyes left.

Sue   Never mind that!

Brett   But she can't . . .

Sue   Put it back!

Brett *throws the angel down.*

Sue   Brett!

Brett *stamps on the angel.*

Silence.

Sue   Not very nice now, was it?

Brett   No.

Sue   Not very nice at all.

Silence.

Well?

Silence.

Brett *picks up the angel.*

Sue   Almost as old as me, that thing.

Brett   So?

Sue   Only comes out once a year.

Brett   Do 'er voice.

Sue   No.

Brett   Want to 'ear 'er voice, do 'er voice.

Sue   I've already told . . .

Brett   Go on.

Sue   She 'ant got no voice.

Silence.

Brett *fixes the angel back on the tree.*

Sue   Good boy.

Silence.

Sue   On the tag, look.

Brett *checks the tag on the present.*

Sue   Well. This is a surprise.

Brett *unwraps the present.*

It's a Sheffield Wednesday football strip.

Sue   Ooh, I say. Very fancy. They are your colours, aren't they? Weren't sure if yer were Wednesday or United.

Brett   United.

Sue   Oh.

Brett   Red n' white.

Sue   Are you sure?

Brett   The blades.

Sue   But I . . .

Brett   Stupid.

Silence.

Sue   Oh. Well, I'm sure I can always get it changed.

Brett   No yer can't.

Sue   I'm sure if I . . .

Brett   Already got one.

Sue   What?

Brett   Stupid.

Sue   Now look . . .

Brett   I get one every season. Wear it t' the match on Saturdays. Wayne Allison's the best, he's the chief. 'Im n' Kozluk.

Sue   I see.

Brett   Michael Tonge's not bad either.

Sue   My Danny used t' support Sheffield Wednesday.

Brett   So?

Sue   He used t' go t' the games back when they were in Division One.

Brett   Shithead.

Sue   What?

Brett   He's a shithead, then. Only shit'eads support Wednesday.

Silence.

Sue Try it on anyway, can't we?

Brett No.

Sue See if it fits.

Brett I don't . . .

Sue Come on . . .

Brett . . . want to . . .

Sue Just a second . . .

Brett Ow!

Sue Don't be such a baby . . .

Brett Geddoff . . .

Sue Brett . . .

Brett Geddoff me!

Sue In a minute.

Brett No.

Sue Let's see yer first.

Brett They're not my team!

Sue Come on . . .

Brett They're not my . . .!

Sue I'll tell yer when they're yer fuckin' team or not, get it on!

Brett But . . .

Sue *slaps* **Brett** *across the face.*

Silence.

Sue *moves to the table and sits.*

Sue *pours wine and drinks.*

Silence.

Brett *gets changed into the football strip.*

Silence.

Sue   There. Didn't hurt now, did it?

Brett   No.

Sue   Let me see.

Silence.

Sue   Well. Don't you look the bonnie prince?

Silence.

Aren't yer havin' a good time?

Brett   No.

Sue   Are you sulkin'?

Brett   No.

Sue   Are you a Grumpus McMumpus?

Silence.

I think you are.

Silence.

Wunt tell on yer Auntie Susan, would yer?

Brett *shrugs.*

Sue   Our little secret.

Brett   You started it.

Sue   What?

Brett   Yer did.

Sue   Don't be . . .

Brett   Only 'ere 'cause they sent me.

Sue   Well, if yer weren't so naughty . . .

Brett Dint want t' come at all.

Sue We can't always have what we want.

Brett I dint.

Sue Then yer'll just 'ave t' make do then, won't yer?

Brett No.

Sue Wunt want to upset yer mother now.

Brett She dunt care.

Sue Wunt want to upset 'er.

Brett She hates your guts.

Sue Now, don't . . .

Brett 'Er and me dad.

Sue Don't be silly.

Brett She does.

Sue She doesn't hate anyone.

Brett I 'eard 'er.

Sue No one hates anyone, Brett, that's a fact, now . . .

Brett Waits inside.

Sue Sit down.

Brett Waits f' yer to go back in when she hangs out line. Dunt like the way yer pick up me sister, she said, says it's rude. Said yer don't hold babies like that, said yer held 'er like a cat. Says she only lets yer do it 'cause yer old. 'Cause yer old n' yer stupid n' yer 'ant got none of yer own.

Silence.

Sue More puddin' if yer want it.

Silence.

'Ave some puddin'.

Brett No.

Sue   Just a slither now, come on.

Brett   Can I use your toilet?

Sue   Come on, Brett.

Brett   Need a wee.

Sue   Don't play . . .

Brett   Need a . . .

Sue   . . . silly beggars with me!

Silence.

Think yer in enough trouble, don't you?

Brett   No.

Sue   Trouble at school.

Brett   Yer wrong.

Sue   Disruptin' classes. Bullyin'. Pickin' on kids half yer size.

Brett   Shuddup.

Sue   Yer mother told me all about it.

Silence.

Give some lad a nose-bleed, dint yer?

Brett   She's lyin'.

Sue   Couldn't believe it when I 'eard. That can't be right, I said.

Brett   Weren't just me.

Sue   Must be mistaken, surely.

Brett   Marcus from two doors down, he's the one who starts it. He does.

Silence.

Sue *refills her glass of wine.*

Sue   Well, I don't know who keeps kickin' my wheelie bin

over every mornin'. Twenty minutes it took me to clean it
all off the road last week.

Silence.

Yer wouldn't know anythin' about that now, would you?

Brett   No.

Sue   Are you sure?

Brett   Shuddup.

Sue   I can always ask yer mother.

Silence.

I'm sure she'd be very interested to hear about that.

Brett   Weren't me.

Sue   Some of us are better at keepin' secrets than others.

Brett   It wasn't.

Sue   Brett . . .

Brett   Why's it always me all the time?

Silence.

Sue   Can't help the way yer feel, poor thing.

Silence.

Sue *pours a glass of brandy and hands it to* **Brett**.

Sue   World dunt revolve round you no more.

Silence.

Brett *hesitates, then sips the brandy.*

Sue   Little baby sister t' think of. Surprised they've got the
time t' play with you no more.

Silence.

Must get very lonely.

Brett   I 'ate 'er.

Sue   What?

Brett Can't even speak.

Sue Bet yer'd like t' give 'em all bloody nose-bleeds given the chance.

Brett Yeah.

Sue I know I would.

Silence.

Can hear everythin' through these walls.

Silence.

Way yer mum n' dad've been arguin' last few month, dread t' think how you must feel.

Silence.

Can't see 'em lastin' much longer, t' tell yer the truth.

Silence.

Know yer can always come to me though, don't yer?

Brett Yeah.

Sue Door's always open.

Brett Yeah.

Sue Yes what?

Brett Mrs Webber, I know.

Silence.

Sue 'Ere.

Sue *gets out of her chair.*

She finds her handbag and takes out her purse.

From the purse **Sue** *takes out a twenty-pound note.*

She hands the note to **Brett**.

Sue Buy yerself somethin' nice. Go on.

Brett *takes the note from* **Sue** *and pockets it.*

Sue   Make up f' the strip.

Silence.

Sue *moves to the tree and takes the angel off.*

Silence.

Sue *moves to* **Brett**, *holding the angel.*

Silence.

Sue (*as the angel*)   'Appy Christmas, Brett.

Silence.

Sue (*as the angel*)   'Appy Christmas, Brett.

Silence.

Sue *hands the angel to* **Brett**.

Sue   Keep 'er in yer bedroom with the others, can't yer?

Brett   Yeah.

Sue   Give 'er a name.

Brett   Mrs Webber.

Sue   That's a nice name.

Silence.

Come 'ere.

Brett   What?

Sue   Come 'ere. Come on.

Silence.

See? That's better int it?

Silence.

Must be tired, poor thing.

Silence.

Expect they'll be wonderin' where yer've got to.

Silence.

Sleep in my Danny's old room.

Brett   Yeah.

Sue   Still got all 'is old England posters on the walls. Might be some players yer recognise.

Silence.

Nip across. Tell 'em how yer feel. Tell 'em yer'd rather stay at yer auntie's, get out from under their feet. Sit in front the telly, couldn't we? Find some cartoons t' watch. Yer'd like that, wunt yer? Bit o' peace. Time t' think.

Silence.

Christ was born on this day.

Silence.

Ask f' yer pyjamas. Any toys yer might want.

Silence.

Brett   Paint 'er some new ones.

Sue   What?

Brett   Felt tips in me drawer. Paint 'er some new eyes, can't we? Paint 'er some new ones so she can see.

Blackout.

Three

Same day. Midnight.

Eddie *sitting in the armchair, watching television.*

On his lap is a basket of nuts. Using a nutcracker, he eats the nuts.

He swigs from a bottle of beer.

He has a black eye.

Silence.

Sue *enters in her nightie, carrying a quilt, sheets and a pillow.*

Sue   Put 'im in your room. Won't hurt for one night.

She proceeds to make **Eddie***'s makeshift bed.*

Sue   Don't know what yer do t' get it in such a state. Found six o' my good coffee cups in there just now. Ashtrays tipped over the floor.

Silence.

Even Danny used t' know when to use the Hoover when he had to.

Silence.

Small wonder yer never get any sleep wi' these sheets. Should put 'em in the bathroom like I asked.

Silence.

This alright for yer?

Eddie   Ay.

Sue   Always grab a towel from out the airin' cupboard.

Silence.

Must be shattered.

Eddie   I am.

Sue   Yer look it.

Silence.

Like t' get an early start. Busy day ahead of us. Said we'd take him along if he wants. He's never been out in Derbyshire before. Thought we might take him over Snake Pass. Long as the car 'olds up. Long as it's not too . . .

Eddie *throws a nut at* **Sue**.

Sue   Eddie . . .

Eddie *throws a nut at* **Sue**.

Sue   Don't do that.

Eddie *throws a nut at* **Sue**.

Sue   Don't do that, Eddie.

Eddie *eats.*

Silence.

Sue *picks up the nuts.*

Sue *puts them back in the basket.*

Silence.

Should take a peek.

Eddie   I'm watchin'.

Sue   Out like a light once 'is 'ead 'it the pillow. Sweetest little thing. Takes yer right back.

Silence.

Take a little peek, Ted, come on.

Eddie   Yer hair's fallin' out.

Sue   What?

Eddie   I've noticed.

Silence.

Sue   Oh. Carry on.

Eddie   Up the Khyber.

Sue   What?

Eddie   *Carry On Up Khyber.*

Sue   Don't raise your voice at me.

Eddie   Shift.

Sue   There's children asleep, fast asleep . . .

Eddie   Fat arse blockin' the sun.

Sue   Turn it down.

Eddie   Yer blockin' the screen!

Sue   The remote, Ted.

Sue *takes the remote and turns the sound down.*

Sue   Give 'im bloody nightmares wi' that racket.

Silence.

Eddie *flicks channels.*

Silence.

Eddie *eats.*

Silence.

Sue   *Spartacus.*

Eddie   Ay.

Silence.

Sue   Eddie.

Silence.

Eddie . . .

Eddie   What?

Sue   Gone midnight already.

Silence.

Can I watch?

Eddie   If yer must.

Sue   Thought we might keep each other company.

Silence.

Sleep in my room if yer'd rather.

Silence.

Moved it all round last week. Put the bed under the window.
Lovely in the mornings with the light shinin' through.

Silence.

Very good, int 'e?

Eddie   What?

Sue   Tony Curtis.

Eddie   'Oo?

Sue   He's very underrated, they say.

Silence.

Fetch the little portable up from the kitchen. Use the extension cable. Sure I can find some room for it on the dresser. Keep each other warm.

Silence.

Yer can smoke.

Eddie   What?

Sue   Open the window a bit. Keep the heatin' on, well . . . Hardly tell the difference, will we?

Eddie   No.

Sue   I don't mind.

Eddie   Thanks.

Sue   Have the fright of his life, 'e finds yer down 'ere in the mornin'. Sprawled out like that. What's 'e goin' t' think, eh?

Eddie *takes a cigarette from his packet.*

Sue   What's he goin' t' think, Ted?

Silence.

Well?

Eddie   Let 'im think.

Sue   Don't be like . . .

Eddie   Leave me alone.

Sue   Eddie . . .

Eddie   Move!

Sue   I've asked you once already . . .

Eddie   Jesus Christ . . .

Sue   Are you comin' t' bed?

Silence.

Eddie *lights the cigarette.*

Silence.

Sue   Want t' watch that, you. Bedbound time yer sixty, way yer carry on. End up like yer father, bloody great hole through yer throat.

Silence.

Don't say I didn't warn yer.

Silence.

Know 'ow restless she gets without 'er dad.

Eddie   What?

Sue   Lucky.

Silence.

Come upstairs with us, can't she? Let 'er sleep on the bed for once. Can't imagine there's much life in 'er now. Not after your carry on.

Eddie   Sue . . .

Sue   Has she even had 'er supper?

Silence.

Ted.

Eddie   What?

Sue   Where is she?

Silence.

The dog, where's the dog?

Silence.

Sue   Yer dint leave the gate open did yer?

Eddie   No.

Sue   Where is she?

Eddie   Go to bed.

Sue   She can't just vanish.

Eddie   She's fine.

Sue   She can't just vanish, Ted.

Eddie   I paid for 'er!

Sue   But . . .

Eddie   She's mine!

Silence.

Eddie *stubs out the cigarette.*

Silence.

Sue   Yer left 'er there.

Eddie   Yes.

Sue   Yer left 'er there.

Silence.

Yer know she dunt like bein' left without 'er basket.

Silence.

Yer know what she's like, Ted, she'll go frantic by 'erself. Leave 'er stranded. Some bloody stranger . . .

Eddie   She's not.

Sue   That's exactly what she is!

Silence.

Eddie   Pamela.

Sue   Fine.

Eddie   'Er name's Pamela.

Sue   Gone all bloody night.

Eddie   It's over.

Sue   What?

Eddie   It's finished.

Sue   What's she done t' yer?

Eddie   Sue . . .

Sue   Yer eye.

Eddie   Let go.

Sue   Above yer eye –

Eddie   Leave it.

Sue   Yer've been fightin'.

Eddie   I knocked it.

Sue   You . . .

Eddie   On the door.

Sue   Which door?

Eddie   Her front door.

Sue   As yer were leavin'?

Eddie   As I was leavin', yes.

Eddie *tries to turn the volume up, using the remote.*

Sue *snatches the remote from his hand and turns the telly off.*

Sue   More of a scratch than a knock.

Eddie   Give it back.

Sue   Couldn't see where you were goin'.

Eddie   No.

Sue   Yer couldn't see.

Eddie   It's possible.

Sue   Yer drunk.

Eddie   . . .

Sue   Yer not drunk. Yer couldn't see where yer were goin'.

Eddie   Look . . .

Sue   Keep secrets from me.

Eddie   I already told . . .

Sue   Yer've tried it on with 'er, 'ant yer?

Eddie *goes to take a nut,*

Sue *knocks the basket of nuts out of his lap.*

Silence.

Mark o' bleedin' Zorro.

Silence.

Sue *gets down on the ground and picks up the nuts one by one, putting them in the basket.*

Silence.

Sue   Wunt be seen dead with the likes o' you.

Eddie   No.

Sue   Woman like 'er.

Silence.

Missed that chance years ago.

Eddie   Sue . . .

Sue   I'm not a bloody fool!

Sue *puts the last of the nuts back in the basket.*

Sue *hands the basket back to* **Eddie**.

Silence.

Sue *moves to the table and pours herself a glass of wine.*

She drinks.

Silence.

Sue   Don't suppose she's had any word?

Eddie   What?

Sue   That husband of hers.

Eddie   No.

Sue   Don't suppose there's any chance . . .

Eddie   She's sellin' up.

Sue   What?

Eddie   Lookin' at some villa.

Sue   What?

Eddie   Spanish villa.

Silence.

On the internet.

Sue   Oh.

Eddie   Reckons she can get work over there.

Sue   Tried t' talk 'er out of it, did yer?

Silence.

Yer know what she's like, Ted.

Silence.

Been the same since we were teenagers, it won't last.
Different bloody story every month, you know that.

Silence.

Might want t' put some TCP on that. Stop it swellin'.

Silence.

Do 'er good. Bit o' sunshine.

Eddie   Ay.

Sue   Damn sight cheaper than over 'ere. Wouldn't say no meself.

Silence.

Can't remember the last time we had an 'oliday.

Silence.

Eddie.

Silence.

Eddie . . .

Eddie   I'm not cryin'.

Silence.

Sue   Come to bed.

Silence.

Just tonight, Ted, please. Come to bed.

Silence.

Sue *moves to the table and sits.*

She pours and drinks more wine.

Silence.

Read any good books?

Silence.

Eddie . . .

Eddie   What?

Sue   'Ant seen any in the bathroom. Thought yer might . . .

Eddie   No.

Sue   I'm readin' somethin'.

Silence.

Ian McEwan. *The Child in Time.*

Silence.

I'm re-readin' it.

Eddie   Oh.

Silence.

Sue   Thought yer might o' dipped into that Sinatra. One 'e got yer f' yer birthday.

Eddie   No.

Sue   Thought yer might've made a start.

Silence.

Been watchin' the news at all?

Silence.

Good t' know they caught 'im. Good t' see 'em steppin' up the pressure. I think it's good.

Silence.

What do you think?

Silence.

There's a Turkish couple taken over the newsagents up the road. They're very pleasant.

Silence.

Have yer met them yet?

Silence.

Back at work on Friday.

Silence.

Go in early.

Silence.

Danny's been on the phone again. Couple o' times. Told 'im yer were flat out on the ouzo. There's no wakin' 'im, I said.

Silence.

He's expectin' yer t' call. Least, 'e was. Got any sense, he'll be in bed by now. They're havin' another outin' tomorrow. She's takin' 'im to 'er mum's in Wiltshire. Show him the stables.

Silence.

She's got a bloody stables. Wants to get him saddled up on one of 'er horses. In this weather.

Silence.

Spoilt cow.

Silence.

Not the type though, is she? They've never mentioned it.

Silence.

Children.

Silence.

Should never 'ave moved down there in the first place. Should never have let 'im go, Ted.

Silence.

Course she'll leave 'im.

Silence.

He'll get cancer.

Silence.

He'll get cancer and she'll leave him.

Silence.

This time next year. The three of us.

Silence.

Number's on side.

Silence.

He's waitin' for a phone call, Ted.

Silence.

Eddie *digs into his pocket.*

Eddie *takes out a small wrapped present.*

Eddie *unwraps the present.*

A jewellery case.

Eddie *opens the jewellery case.*

Silence.

Sue   Eddie . . .

Eddie   Turn the light off.

Sue   Look at me.

Eddie   Turn it . . .

Sue   Look at me, Ted.

Silence.

Be up for retirement in a few year.

Silence.

Take 'er the vet's.

Eddie   What?

Sue   Tell 'em she's sick. Tell 'em she's not been eatin'.

Silence.

Only take a few minutes. Won't feel a thing.

Silence.

Bury 'er in the garden.

Silence.

Yer can't go back there.

Eddie   What?

Sue   Yer goin' back there.

Eddie   No.

Sue   Well, go on!

Eddie   Does it look like I'm . . .?

Sue   Bended bloody knees!

Eddie   I'm not . . .

Sue   Yer in love with 'er, aren't yer?

Silence.

Well, aren't yer?

Silence.

Bastard.

Eddie   Ay.

Sue   Careless bastard, waste my . . .

The phone rings.

Silence.

Pick it up.

Silence.

Talk to 'im.

Silence.

Talk to 'im, go on.

Silence.

Your fuckin' child, Eddie Webber, pick up the phone!

The phone stops ringing.

Long silence.

Sue *growls at* **Eddie**.

Sue *snarls at* **Eddie**.

Sue *circles* **Eddie**, *growling and snarling.*

Sue *barks at* **Eddie**.

Sue *growls and snarls and barks at* **Eddie**.

Silence.

Sue *sits at the table.*

She tries to pour more wine. There is only a trickle.

Silence.

Eddie *takes the necklace out of the case.*

Eddie *moves to* **Sue**.

Eddie *ties the necklace round* **Sue**'s *neck.*

Silence.

Eddie   Take it off.

Silence.

Yer nightie. Let me see yer.

Silence.

Eddie *returns to the armchair.*

Silence.

Eddie *takes off his shirt.*

Eddie *takes off his shoes.*

Eddie *takes off his trousers.*

Eddie *climbs into his bed.*

Silence.

Brett *enters, in his pyjamas. He holds the angel.*

Silence.

Brett   Can't sleep.

Silence.

Can't sleep.

Silence.

Brett *tugs at* **Sue***'s arm.*

Brett   Can't sleep, I 'eard noises.

Blackout.

Four

One year later.

A beach in Fuerteventura, the Canary Islands. Christmas Day.

Bright and sunny.

Two sunbeds and a beach umbrella.

Sue *lays on her front on the sunbed in her swimming costume.*

Silence.

Sue *turns over onto her back.*

She shuts her eyes.

Silence.

Sue *covers her eyes from the light.*

Silence.

Sue *opens her eyes, slowly sits up.*

Sue *looks and finds the bottle of sunlotion.*

Sue *squirts the sunlotion and rubs it into her arms.*

Silence.

Sue *gets up and moves to the beach umbrella.*

Sue *tries to put the beach umbrella up* . . .
She can't.

Sue *tries again to put the beach umbrella up* . . .
She can't.

Silence.

Sue *lays back down on the sunbed, on her front.*

Five

A short time later.

The beach umbrella is up.

Eddie *and* **Sue** *lay on their backs on the sunbeds.*

Eddie *is wet from the sea, with a towel over his legs.*

Silence.

Sue   Felt that breeze.

Eddie   What?

Sue   The breeze.

Silence.

Sue   There.

Eddie   What?

Sue   Didn't yer feel it?

Eddie   No.

Sue   It came back again.

Silence.

Don't fancy that dinner tonight, d' yer?

Eddie   Ay.

Sue   Turkey roast for three hundred guests. Dunt bear thinkin' about.

Silence.

Passed that place last night. In the old town.

Eddie   If yer want.

Sue   Looked good from the outside.

Silence.

Open our presents, can't we? Take 'em with us.

Silence.

Swim far?

Eddie   What?

Sue   Did yer swim very far?

Eddie   Not really.

Sue   Couldn't see yer.

Eddie   T' the rock n' back.

Sue   That's nice.

Six

A short time later.

Eddie *rubs suntan lotion onto* **Sue**'s *back.*

Sue   Make sure yer do me shoulders.

Eddie   Plastered with the stuff.

Sue   What?

Eddie   Yer plastered.

Silence.

Sue   Not there.

Eddie What?

Sue Left a bit.

Silence.

Up a bit.

Eddie How's that?

Sue More. Squirt some more on.

Eddie *gently pulls the straps from* **Sue***'s shoulders.*

Eddie *squirts lotion in his palms.*

Eddie *rubs lotion on* **Sue***'s shoulders.*

Sue That's it.

Seven

A short time later.

Sue *and* **Eddie** *sat up on their sunbeds.*

They both drink from bottles of fizzy orange pop, using straws.

Cliff Richard's 'Mistletoe and Wine' can be heard in the distance.

Silence.

Sue Can you 'ear that?

Pause.

It's Cliff.

Eddie What?

Sue They're playin' bloody Cliff.

Silence.

Eddie Someone's idea of a joke.

Sue Bit o' fun.

Silence.

She would've loved it 'ere.

Eddie   What?

Sue   All this space.

Silence.

Sue *lays down on her sunbed.*

Silence.

Eddie *finds his cigarettes.*

He takes one out of the pack and lights it.

Sue   Very strong them, Ted.

Eight

A short time later.

Sue *sunbathing, alone.*

*A young boy/***Brett**, *building a sandcastle with a bucket and spade.*

Silence.

Sue *sits up.*

Silence.

Sue *watches the young boy.*

Silence.

Sue *lays back down.*

Nine

A short time later.

Eddie *and* **Sue** *sunbathing.*

Silence.

Eddie   Not of the same calibre now.

Sue   Who?

Silence.

Who isn't? – What?

Silence.

Sue   Who?

Silence.

Did you say somethin'?

Eddie   Ronnie O'Sullivan.

Sue   What about 'im?

Silence.

Eddie   Cliff Thorburn.

Sue   What?

Eddie   Ray Reardon.

Silence.

'Urricane 'Iggins.

Silence.

Jimmy White.

Silence.

Went t' see it, dint we?

Sue   Oo?

Eddie   Steve Davis.

Sue   Oh.

Eddie   Went the semi-final.

Ten

A short time later.

Eddie *sunbathing.*

Sue *sitting on the edge of the sunbed, dusting down her flip-flops.*

Silence.

Sue   You alright?

Silence.

Sue *puts on her flip-flops.*

Sue   Goin' for a paddle.

Sue *pulls herself to her feet.*

Sue   Won't be long.

Sue *takes her sarong.*

Eddie *sits up.*

Sue *ties the sarong round her waist.*

Silence.

Eddie   Don't go too far.

Blackout.